Becoming a Learner

Realizing the Opportunity of Education

Second Edition

Matthew L. Sanders

macmillan learning
curriculum solutions

ISBN 978-1-5339-0406-5

Macmillan Learning Curriculum Solutions
14903 Pilot Drive
Plymouth, MI 48170
www.macmillanlearning.com

Sanders 0406-5 F18

macmillan learning
curriculum solutions

Sustainability
Hayden-McNeil's standard paper stock uses a minimum of 30% post-consumer waste. We offer higher % options by request, including a 100% recycled stock. Additionally, Hayden-McNeil Custom Digital provides authors with the opportunity to convert print products to a digital format. Hayden-McNeil is part of a larger sustainability initiative through Macmillan Learning. Visit http://sustainability.macmillan.com to learn more.

bedford/st. martin's • hayden-mcneil
w.h. freeman • worth publishers

About the Author

Matthew Sanders is Associate Professor of Communication Studies at Utah State University, and holds a PhD in Communication from the University of Colorado at Boulder. He has a long-standing interest in helping students improve their college experience, and enjoys working closely with the orientation and first-year experience programs at Utah State. In addition to his writing and speaking about the college experience, he also teaches classes and publishes research on the topics of leadership, organizations, the nonprofit sector, and pedagogy. He can be reached at matt.sanders@usu.edu.

To Julie

Table of Contents

Preface to the Second Edition

Most independently published books have a very short and localized lifespan. *Becoming a Learner* has been very different. It needed to be published independently because the manuscript had demand before it could go through a traditional publishing process. Then it quickly gained traction among students and teachers. Now in just a few years, its use in programs and classrooms has spread quickly. Orientation, first-year experience, and academic programs in large public universities, community colleges, land-grant universities, and private liberal arts colleges have used this book to help students better understand and take advantage of their college experience. With this success, it was time to create an improved second edition with a traditional publisher.

The success of *Becoming a Learner* speaks to how much students and teachers want a simple and straightforward way to understand and talk about the purpose of college. I have learned both in my classes before this book was published and in a variety of settings since, that students can find significant meaning and motivation when they are given the time and space to consider what it means to educate the whole self and the importance of becoming a broadly educated person.

The most common response to this book from students has been that no one has really ever talked to them about the purpose of higher education and the value of the whole degree. They were told to go to college, and that it was important for getting a good job. For many students, the message of this book feels exciting and empowering, resonating with what they hope college will be. For some, this message can feel frustrating at first because it challenges their view of higher education. Regardless of the reaction, when students tell me that after reading and considering the message of *Becoming a Learner* they found greater focus, purpose, and meaning in their education, I feel grateful that at least one of the answers to the vexing problem of helping students persist to graduation doesn't require an expensive fix or curriculum overhaul.

Becoming a Learner certainly isn't the only thing that helps students continue on to graduation, but it is the first message they need to hear. Knowing the *why* of college makes a significant difference to students and helps change their mindset about what college is, what they need to do to be successful, and who they can become. Ironically, when students do this and engage their studies accordingly, they actually better align themselves with what employers will expect of them when they graduate. As a result, their career prospects and potential for success increase. And once students see themselves as learners, all the other good work that colleges and universities do to help students succeed can have more impact.

There are several revisions to note in this second edition. First, I have improved and clarified the framing of the book's thesis and other key themes throughout the book. These small revisions are most extensive in the Introduction and Chapter 1, but similar changes and elaborations can be found in the other chapters. These revisions respond to questions from students and are meant to sharpen and clarify the arguments I make in ways that I hope will improve understanding. Second, the section on communication skills in Chapter 2 has been revised and reframed to better match the research showing how important communication competence is to employers. Third, I have added a new "distracting conversation" to Chapter 3 that challenges the assumption that college is just about getting a piece of paper. Finally, I added additional reflection questions to Chapter 5. Overall, I hope this second edition even more successfully helps students recognize the opportunity that their education offers them and helps them take full advantage of it.

Matt Sanders
February 2018

Introduction

When I was a sophomore in college, one of my professors challenged the way I looked at the world. He guided his literature course by a simple saying: *The hardest thing for you to know is the thing you think you already know.*[1] From that course I learned the value of re-examining what seems obvious or appears to be common sense in order to change the way I understand the circumstances around me or to help me remember why I think and behave the way I do.

This is the task that I am asking you to take on as you read this book.

Education and learning are so familiar to us that it's easy to think we understand what they are. Formal education becomes part of life in preschool or kindergarten and we grow up with it. By the time we reach college, we believe we know how the education system works and why we are learning. Yet, we rarely step back and look at education anew to remember its purpose and goals. As a result, many so-called commonsense ways of understanding and pursuing a college education are actually guided by misconceptions and misunderstandings that limit learning and keep us from reaching our potential.

My experience both as a student and as a teacher has shown me that too many college students go about their education in ways that work against their own goals and interests because nobody has helped them carefully think through what college is and what it's designed to do. Given the amount of time, money, and effort that you will invest to earn a degree, it is important to carefully reconsider the purpose of higher education and to question commonsense understandings of what college is and how to complete college successfully.

This book is not meant to offer a definitive explanation of the history and purposes of higher education. Nor is it meant to offer quick fixes for the many challenges you will face or to provide how-to instructions for classroom learning and study skills.

Rather, my purpose is to offer a broad philosophy of learning that will enable you to make more sense out of everything you do in college. I am confident that when you focus on becoming a learner, you will improve your college experience. I hope these ideas will serve as a starting point for a new kind of conversation that will help you take full advantage of your opportunity for higher education.

CHAPTER 1

When Learning Job Skills Is Not Enough

During my senior year of college, one of my professors told me about a meeting he had with a news agency director. During that meeting my professor asked the director how many journalism majors he typically hired. The director's reported response completely changed the way I thought about college and learning. He said, "I don't often hire journalism majors. Many times I hire philosophy, political science, or English majors. I can teach anybody how to write a good news story. I'm looking for people who can think critically and analytically, people who are problem solvers."[2]

This story bothered me for two reasons. First, I couldn't understand how people could get jobs doing something outside of their college majors. I had assumed that students always got jobs related to their majors. Second, and more importantly, I wondered if I was like the person who'd gotten the job because he was a critical and analytical thinker or if I was like the one who'd learned the necessary job skills but still didn't measure up. I hoped I was the critical thinker, but to be honest, I wasn't sure. And that troubled me.

A few months later, I heard a similar story during a teaching seminar. The presenter told of a friend who'd been touted for years as one of the best recruiters in the computer science industry. Everyone he recruited turned out to be an excellent computer scientist. He was, however, reluctant to share the secret of his success because he said that nobody ever followed his advice: "Hire honors history majors instead of C+ computer science majors."

1

For me, these stories raised an important question: If job skills are not the only or most important outcome of a college education, then what is the purpose of earning a degree? After months of thinking about these stories and reflecting on my own experiences in college, I finally figured out my answer: *The primary purpose of college isn't learning a specific set of professional skills; the primary purpose of college is to become a learner.* In other words, the kind of thinker, problem solver, and person you become as a result of your education is much more important than what you learn how to do.

What the news agency director and the computer science recruiter understand is that job skills—by themselves—are not enough. They are merely one aspect of the array of knowledge and abilities required to be successful in any given profession. What the news director, the recruiter, and nearly every employer are most interested in is who the graduate has *become,* not just the specific set of professional skills he or she has learned. Every national and local survey of what college graduates need to know and do upon graduation show that employers want well-rounded, broadly educated people who are critical thinkers, careful problem solvers, and effective communicators.[3]

To do this, you must develop creativity, intelligence, and your personal capacity to work and learn—qualities that become part of "who you are." These abilities never become outdated or obsolete. Once a part of your character, they are not easily forgotten. And the need for learners with these character traits is not restricted to any single course, major, or profession.

In saying this, I am not suggesting that professionally focused learning isn't important, useful, or needed. Acquiring practical skills and gaining professional experience during college is important. It's just not the *most* important learning you will do or the *only* learning that matters.[4] Employers will evaluate you primarily on who you have become as a result of your college education and on your capacity to continue learning and growing. Even in professionally oriented majors, who you are still matters more than what you can do because it speaks to your long-term potential for success.

What I am suggesting is that you primarily focus on who you are becoming as a learner in all aspects of your education. Focusing *solely* on professional skills is shortsighted and actually works against your own best interests. In contrast, concentrating on who you are becoming allows you to recognize the need for developing professional skills without overlooking the most important and primary product of your education—you.

This perspective also allows you to recognize that the purpose of your education is much more than simply securing employment. You are not in college to become an employee. Look at your college or university's mission statement: You are in college to become a more capable person and contributing citizen.[5] Who you become in college will not only have a significant impact on your career but also on your family, your community, and every organization and group in which you participate.[6]

An Invitation to a New Kind of Conversation

The way you talk about education and learning matters.[7] The words and stories you use to describe and make sense of college will either orient you toward taking advantage of your opportunities or they will work against you by obscuring the most important outcomes of higher education. How you talk about your college education influences what you deem useful or useless, important or unimportant. Your conversations will determine the kind of effort and attention you devote to your studies.

Unfortunately, most conversations about college and learning seem to revolve around acquiring job skills and focus on the idea of "doing." Take, for example, the following questions that nearly everyone repeatedly asks:

- "What are you going to do with that major?"
- "How is this class going to help me when I get a job?"
- "When am I ever going to use this knowledge in the real world?"

While this kind of thinking might seem natural and legitimate, these are actually loaded questions. People who engage in conversations about such questions usually insist that any major, class, or assignment be directly related to something that can be immediately applied to a job. Therefore, answers to these questions must argue against the steady and careful academic development and personal growth that determine who you become, give you the character and abilities employers want most, and serve as the foundation of your career. These are also the wrong questions to ask because they will give you an incredibly narrow focus on the entry-level job you will get after graduation, which is likely the be the least interesting and exciting of your career.[8]

Although the idea of "doing" does matter, if you let a focus on job skills dominate your conversations and actions, you will be unnecessarily confused about and frustrated with college. So much of what you do in college, such as doing research and taking general education classes, is designed to help you become a more intelligent, capable, understanding, aware, and competent person—regardless of your major.

The purpose of this book is to introduce you to a more helpful way of thinking and talking about college and learning that will enable you to take full advantage of your education. I invite you to carefully reconsider what we so often think of as common sense ideas about the purpose and outcomes of college and embrace a new kind of conversation that focuses on who you are becoming and your long-term personal and professional success.

CHAPTER 2

Becoming a Learner

Thinking that every major, class, or assignment should connect to a specific job or professional skill distracts us from recognizing the primary purpose of education: to become a learner. As a result, we often overlook our most important and valuable learning experiences and fail to take full advantage of the opportunities a college education offers. Too often we get so caught up answering questions about what we will do with our majors and what value a particular class or assignment holds for our professional careers that we forget that the most important outcome of learning is who we become as a result of our education.

Brian McCoy is the CEO of a successful building supply company. In a commencement speech at Texas State University, he explained that asking "What do I need to do to be successful?" is misguided. Instead, he argued, we should ask, "Who do we need to become to be successful?"[9] He's right.

From the perspective of becoming, everything you do in college matters. Everything counts—both inside the classroom and out.

And it's not only *what* you do that counts; it's also *how* you do it.

Who you become as a result of your education is the culmination of your everyday actions and efforts. Over time, as you participate in a variety of activities and take an assortment of courses, you change and grow. You become a different person. It is the steadiness of your work ethic, your daily diligence in doing what is expected of you, the manner in which you handle yourself in social situations, how you deal with setbacks and challenges, the extent to which you think carefully and critically, and your ability to learn new and challenging ideas that will determine who you become. However, there is no guarantee that you'll become a learner just by getting a college degree. That depends on you. You can go through college and graduate and actually not improve or even become worse in terms of your character, intelligence, and personal capacity.[10] Just getting by, working the system, cramming, cheating, procrastinating, avoiding responsibility, making excuses, and doing the least amount of work possible will over time result in your becoming lazy, unethical, unable to clearly reason through difficult problems, and unprepared to be excellent at whatever you do. A person who has developed those characteristics certainly isn't in high demand anywhere.

On the other hand, consistently striving for excellence, working to your potential, steadily completing your assignments, working hard, meeting challenges, being prepared, asking for help, and overcoming mistakes and failures will result in your becoming the kind of person who has the ability to excel in any environment.

When you focus on who you are becoming, you will recognize that college is a time of preparation. How you take advantage of your time and opportunities determines the kind of person you become.

You don't suddenly become a learner when you don a cap and gown at graduation. Too many students mistakenly think that everyone is equal at graduation because each has a diploma. Although it is true that you will have the same diploma as others, you will not be the same person as your fellow graduates. Each of you will have different skills, abilities, and especially potential.

It's not just *that* you completed a degree; it is *how* you earned your degree and the cumulative effects of your education that matter.

Why Becoming Matters

When your conversations and attitudes revolve around whether or not your major or classes are building enough professional skills, you overlook three important realities of the world you'll enter after graduation: (1) Your degree doesn't guarantee you a good job. (2) You are going to forget much of what you learn. (3) Many of the job skills you learn in college will become obsolete.

Reality 1: Your Degree Doesn't Guarantee You a Good Job

After his first two years of college, my dad took a leave of absence to return home and marry my mom. While my mom finished her degree, my dad got a job loading railroad cars at a shipping warehouse. When the loading supervisor and warehouse manager found out that my dad had attended two years of college, they transferred him to the office and gave him a job as a clerk. No questions were asked about what classes he'd taken or what skills he had. He had been to college, and that was good enough.

For a long time, people who went to college did so assuming that if they worked hard, did well, and graduated, they would get a good job.[11] For previous generations that was true. Those conditions, however, don't exist for you. Regardless of your major, there is no guarantee that you will find a high-paying job immediately after graduation doing exactly what you'd hoped to do in your chosen profession.

I've seen many bright, capable graduates struggle for a while before finding the kind of employment they wanted. I've watched very accomplished students, many with professional experience in their fields, take unpaid part-time positions or internships or accept low-paying jobs in order to get additional experience and to prove themselves to future employers. Even those who get the kinds of corporate jobs that many students seem to covet still have to work very hard to prove that they can learn and thrive in the workplace. As I've watched this process in others and reflected on my own experience, this fact is repeatedly affirmed: Upon graduation your biggest asset is your potential and your ability to learn, not your expertise.

As the opportunity for higher education grows both in the United States and globally, more people will graduate with college degrees than ever before. At the same time some predict that within only a few years approximately two-thirds of the jobs in the United States will require at least an associate's degree.[12] This suggests that both now and in the future a college degree may make you less unique. Yet, at the same time it will be even more essential in securing employment. In many cases your degree will serve as a credential that will enable you to be *considered* for employment. The kind of learner you have become will be what distinguishes you from everyone else.

Reality 2: You Are Going to Forget Much of What You Learn

I don't remember much of the detail from the approximately 50 classes I took as an undergraduate. I can only tell you about a number of broad ideas and general perspectives. Research shows that over time many people forget significant amounts of the information and ideas they've learned, particularly when that learning isn't immediately connected to something personally meaningful.[13] Of course we don't need research to tell us that months or years after a class we won't remember most of the details we were required to learn. This lack of long-term recall, however, doesn't mean our learning was pointless.

So what is the point of taking so many classes?

Remember, society doesn't hold a college degree in high esteem because you have memorized facts about economics, studied the processes of photosynthesis, or remembered the quadratic equation. Rather, the standing that comes with a college degree lies in the assumption that you have developed an appreciation for the influence of economics on contemporary concerns and recognize the value of scientific knowledge in shaping society.

Companies aren't going to hire you because you took courses in philosophy and English and learned to write research papers. They do, however, seek job candidates who have developed an ability to understand, critique, and make arguments that are logically sound. They want employees who know how to identify important questions, collect and analyze information, and develop informed conclusions.

Thus the reason for taking so many classes is not only to broaden your knowledge—the stated goal of the university—but also to develop you into a person who can reason, think deeply and creatively, and be a lifelong learner.

What will you retain from your classes?

You will retain the most important thing—who you have become as a result of your studies. For example, I don't remember many details about technical writing that I learned as a senior. However, I do remember what it was like to develop a proposal for a project, gather the resources and research necessary to complete it, create a draft, get feedback for improvement from my professor and classmates, revise my manuscript, and finally submit it for evaluation. I remember how hard I worked, how much effort it took, how I felt after receiving feedback, and how hard it was to deal with the obstacles of completing a large assignment. I remember the sense of accomplishment I felt when I was finished, knowing that I had the capacity to do something as complex and difficult as that project. This learning created a foundation for successfully taking on larger projects after I graduated.

I do, therefore, remember some important things that I learned in my technical writing class, but those things were not necessarily the terms and concepts that could be put on a final exam. They were the things that gave me a foundation for thinking like a writer and the confidence to complete a difficult, complex project.

So rather than assuming that specific coursework is the most important aspect of a college education, I suggest that you focus on the learning process itself. For example, you can take multiple history courses and learn how to analyze and evaluate people and events while gaining an appreciation for the importance of history in helping you understand current problems. Or you can slide through those same courses—avoiding careful reading, cramming for exams, doing sloppy work at the last minute, and complaining about how you would rather be doing something else—and gain nothing.

Mastering the process of learning through study, analysis, and experimentation is much more important than the details of what you learn.

Reality 3: Many of the Job Skills You Learn in College Will Become Obsolete

In a speech to business students in 2008 at the University of Colorado at Boulder, Peter Behrendt—a successful engineer, CEO, and venture capitalist—told students not to worry excessively about the technical skills in their chosen fields.[14] As I listened, I thought that advice sounded odd coming from an engineer.

Next this 40-year technology veteran asked the audience to think about the rate at which knowledge develops and technology changes. He asked, "How many times has the amount of space that it takes to electronically store data decreased over the past 40 years?" The students offered various guesses, all of which were far too small. The answer: one billion. It used to take thousands of square feet to store what now fits easily on the tip of your finger.[15]

Thus, the specific professional skills that he'd learned in college about how to store data electronically were obsolete by the time he'd graduated. Knowing this, he suggested that students learn broadly across a number of disciplines in addition to studying the technical aspects of their field.

Peter Behrendt's advice holds true for each field of study and for every career. The way we do things now will change and will probably change quickly. The dramatic rate of technological change means that whatever technical or industry-specific skills you learn in college probably won't last even a few years, let alone a career. This is why Behrendt encouraged students to not be excessively concerned about technical skills. Instead, he encouraged students to also develop excellent communication skills, learn another language, develop a global perspective, learn how to ask good questions, and develop zero tolerance for unethical behavior.

Once again, I emphasize that this does not mean that you should avoid learning technical or professional skills in college. Those skills are important. They can help you get your first job and will enable you to develop your ability to learn in a particular field. However, you should not be *overly* worried about them to the point where you make job skills the sole focus of college. What you need to do is recognize that their usefulness and value probably won't last very long.

Thinking ahead to the entirety of your future career and life, you will spend most of your time working with technologies that haven't yet been invented. You'll help solve complex problems that don't currently exist. And both your professional work and community engagement will respond to social, cultural, and economic conditions that haven't arisen. If that doesn't sound realistic to you, just ask anyone who started their career 40 years ago, and they can tell you exactly how this has happened to them.

Your ability to learn how to learn will be what takes you through the countless developments and changes that you will deal with in your work and in society. By recognizing this, you can focus on your development as a learner, which will be more lasting and applicable in all your future endeavors.

Outcomes of Becoming

When you focus on who you are becoming, you will recognize important outcomes of your education that others often overlook. You will see results that are not always directly reflected in grades. These outcomes are distinct from professional job skills because they incorporate broad abilities, personal character traits, and ways of thinking. These qualities are transferable from job to job as well as from career to career. They never become obsolete or outdated, and they can be learned in any discipline or field of study.

And what are these vital qualities? Creativity, the ability to think critically, excellent communication skills, and an exceptional character.

Creativity

Creativity expert Ken Robinson defines creativity as "the process of having original ideas that have value."[16] He explained that research on creativity illustrates that when we are very young, we are extremely creative; as we get older, we lose that creativity.[17] Some, like Ken Robinson, argue that formal education saps the active, exploring, questioning nature of our minds. And they may be right. We are too often told to listen, take notes, and memorize information. Yet when we graduate, begin careers, and get involved in our communities, we are expected to be creative, solve problems, or do something original.[18]

I recognize that some college classes provide little room for originality. Even so, you can take opportunities to be creative both inside and outside the classroom. You can seek out courses, teachers, projects, and activities that will help you develop your creative capacities.

Remember, creativity isn't just confined to art or dance or music. Creativity is possible in every field of study and in all learning environments.[19] Anything that requires you to develop original work or to form your own conclusions can help you develop a creative mind. Sometimes the key to finding opportunities simply lies in asking for permission to do things in a different way.

Critical Thinking

A successful engineer explained to me the importance of critical thinking as an outcome of a college education. He said the world pays you to solve problems. If the only problem you can solve is something extremely simple, you can get paid for it. But the pay won't be much, and you can easily be replaced. If the problem you can solve is to save a life, facilitate collaboration, run a company, develop technology, or something else that is complex or requires expertise, then you become hard to replace and much more valuable.[20]

To be a problem solver, you need to learn how to think critically—a quality that many people consider to be the primary purpose and most important outcome of a college education.[21] Critical thinking is not primarily concerned with knowing the right answers. Instead, critical thinkers master the art of asking good questions in order to solve complex problems.

In business and politics, for example, we often suffer from a lack of critical thinkers. Too many people in these areas come up with solutions based on what they already know or on what will seem "safe" or familiar to their customers, investors, or constituents. Unfortunately, many of the problems we face in our organizations and in our society deal with new and ambiguous conditions that have no clear answers and that cannot be successfully addressed in the same old ways.

In contrast, a critical thinker is able to look at a problem from multiple perspectives, consider contrasting ideas, understand differing arguments, gather good information, and then develop informed conclusions. You must recognize that every new subject, class, paper, or assignment gives you the opportunity to think carefully, ask good questions, and hone your critical thinking skills. When you do, you prepare yourself to become a problem solver.

Communication Skills

Communicating and working effectively with others is considered by nearly all employers to be the most important ability that college graduates need to develop.[22] This means being able to work well with those who see the world differently than you do, come from different nationalities and cultures, or have differing experiences or expertise. Communication seems pretty easy when you're surrounded by people who are like you and when the problems you're solving are simple. But the true measure of competent communicators is how they manage conflict and difference and their ability to bring people with different ideas and experiences together.

Your success depends upon your ability to build and maintain positive, trusting relationships. College provides you with endless opportunities to interact with all kinds of people under many different circumstances. How you communicate with your teachers, peers, roommates, family, and friends helps you develop your communication skills. In every group project, study session, club, class, and conversation with a professor, you are learning to build relationships and work effectively with others. Some of this learning will come from success and positive outcomes. Some of this learning will come from disagreements, conflict, and failure. Regardless of how it comes, it is valuable experience if you learn from it.

Therefore, how you interact with your teachers, advisors, peers, mentors, and others is extremely important. When you graduate from college, you will have spent several years communicating and collaborating with others. Having difficult conversations with a professor about a grade, asking for help when you are confused, and working with your classmates on projects offers you the opportunity to develop competence as a communicator.

If you only focus on grades and developing professional skills, you are likely to miss out on this essential learning. And without strong communication skills, your ability to work successfully with others and accomplish your goals diminishes significantly.

So seek to develop relationships with your professors, learn to ask for feedback and help, continually improve your ability to work effectively with groups, and increase your capacity to appreciate differences and manage conflict.

Character

Character is the sum of qualities that influences *how* you accomplish tasks and achieve goals. These qualities can include a good work ethic, dependability, and honesty. When you focus on who you are becoming in college, the things that will matter most will be how you studied, learned, and completed your work. This focus will build depth of character, a depth that will help you be successful in whatever you do.

When you graduate you should be able to do much more than you were capable of doing when you began college. Your personal capacity and work ethic should be significantly expanded, and you should be ready to stretch yourself even further as you tackle the many opportunities and challenges that await you.

Unfortunately, some college students try to do as little as possible and avoid challenging situations. It can be tempting to think it's smart to figure out ways to work less and to find ways to get a good grade with the least amount of effort. This trap is easy to fall into if you assume that the grade—and not who you become—is the only thing that matters. While it is a good idea to be careful about taking on too much work, your personal capacity will not increase if you avoid stretching yourself. Instead, you should go above and beyond what is expected of you. Don't shy away from doing hard things. Even though hard work can't always be graded, your efforts will always pay off in terms of who you are becoming.

Your character is also influenced by your integrity and your ability to complete tasks on time. Are you honest on all of your tests and assignments, and do you complete them when they are due? Learners understand that they need to do what is expected of them, when it is expected of them, and to do their own work.

Every ethical employer expects you to be able to work hard, meet your obligations, and be honest. In short, your employers will expect you to have depth of character. You will find the same expectations in your personal and community relationships as well. Learners know that such abilities aren't turned on and off like a switch. These abilities are developed and practiced over time and become ways of living in the world. If you develop a lazy and dishonest character in college, you will be that way in your work situations and in your personal life. But if you become a person of high character, others will trust you, enabling you to be successful even in the middle of challenging circumstances.

From Student to Learner

When you understand that the primary purpose of college is to become a learner, you see learning in a new light. Now it's no longer only about what happens in the classroom. Instead, learning becomes something that you're doing all the time. It never stops.

Your learning objectives also change. You move away from an exclusive focus on grades and begin to focus on how your education is transforming you into someone better. You begin to measure your success by how you see and engage the world differently and how your understanding and perspectives expand.

This approach highlights a significant problem with the way many people engage education—passively sitting back and waiting to be taught. Perhaps this point is best illustrated by this question often asked by students who are frustrated with an assignment or uninterested in taking a class: "What exactly do I have to do to get an A?" This question usually implies that they want to do the least amount of work—and therefore learning—in order to get the desired grade.

From the perspective of becoming, being a passive student actually works against you and your desires for success. To get out of this passive stance, I suggest dropping the label of "student" and adopting the label of "learner." Although simply replacing the word doesn't guarantee a change in behavior, speaking differently about how to engage learning—and understanding that difference—can change the way you think about and pursue your education.

To get the most out of your education, you must stop seeing yourself as a student with all the passive and amateur connotations that word can imply. Instead, you must see yourself as a learner who is active, courageous, hardworking, and energized. The following table summarizes the differences between the attitudes and behaviors of students and learners.

STUDENT	LEARNER
Waits to be directed	Seeks out opportunities
Learns for the test	Learns for understanding
Is externally motivated	Is internally motivated
Avoids challenging situations	Seeks challenging situations
Sees learning as an obligation	Sees learning as an opportunity
Learns to do	Learns to learn

Let me elaborate on this distinction with an example. As an undergraduate teaching assistant for a communication theory course, I met both students and learners. Every semester each student was required to write six short papers and take two written exams. The professor told the class members that he'd left the topics of the papers open so they could write about the theories they were most interested in and the ones they understood best. The overall guidelines for the papers were these: be creative, be organized, and think critically.

Most of the students were not used to this type of freedom and responsibility. Some seemed to enjoy it, but others really disliked it. Many who disliked it became frustrated with the open-ended challenge to be creative and to write about what they found interesting. The learners, however, thrived; the freedom to think critically and be creative energized them. Their abilities improved with each succeeding paper, and they earned high grades in the class. Those who remained frustrated with the assignments didn't excel. They blamed their struggles on the professor's teaching style, on not having multiple-choice exams, or on not having assigned paper topics.

In all the classes I have taught since that time, the same pattern has played out. Those who have adopted the mindset of a learner thrive, even through challenges and setbacks. Those who act as passive students coast along, never fully realizing the possibilities for growth and development as a learner.

Now, I understand that being a learner isn't easy and doesn't always come naturally in an education system that often conditions us to be passive. I believe every person who has attended college has played the roles of both student and learner. My own successes and failures were largely determined by the role I adopted. Yet my experience has taught me that we can decide to become learners who actively pursue knowledge and understanding. And that decision—simply choosing to act as a learner—can enable you to grow and improve in all of your learning opportunities.

Making this choice, however, doesn't mean we are always either one or the other. These labels represent sets of behaviors that we work toward developing and enacting. And we are most often some mixture of a student and learner at any given point in our lives depending on how we approach the challenges and opportunities in front of us. That is why it's never too late in your education to embrace the learner's mindset. Whenever you begin the process of becoming a learner, you will do things differently, see your education differently, and find new motivations.

Therefore, striving to be a learner gives you great power. You gain tremendous control over how you learn and who you become. When you break the mold of a passive student and become a learner, you can become more and more successful—no matter how good or bad your educational opportunities and circumstances, no matter how competent your professors, no matter your intellectual abilities. You increase and expand your successes because you do not wait for someone else to make your education better. You take responsibility for who you are becoming.

CHAPTER 3

Distracting Conversations

In order to take full advantage of the opportunity of a college education, we must recognize the kinds of conversations that distract us from focusing on becoming a broadly educated, capable learner. Conversations that sidetrack us from this purpose are founded in some of our most commonsense assumptions about the objectives of a college education. We can hear these conversations in classrooms, homes, the media, and from government leaders.[23] Yet when evaluated carefully, these assumptions largely ignore the importance of who we are becoming as a result of our learning and the role of a broad-based education in personal and professional success. Please carefully consider these conversations and think about how much they influence your own assumptions and attitudes about college and learning.

"I'm going to college so I can get a good job."

There's no question that earning a college degree significantly increases your potential to find a better job than you could get without one. Research clearly shows that over a lifetime, college graduates have access to better-paying jobs and on average make significantly more money than those without a degree.[24] There are notable exceptions, but for every exception there are thousands of examples that support this research.

Although we know that college graduates generally find higher paying jobs and have a lower rate of unemployment, it's important to remember what I explained before: Do not mistake a college education for job training. When college is viewed simply as professional training and obtaining immediately applicable job skills, much of the required general education coursework, assignments, and research becomes frustrating and doesn't make sense. This in turn generates incorrect assumptions that cause you to overlook some of your most important learning experiences.

Again, the *primary* purpose of higher education in the United States has never been to simply develop workers and teach them job skills but rather to help them mature into capable and contributing members of society who can govern themselves and contribute to the common good through entrepreneurship, gainful employment, and community engagement. In other words, the primary purpose of education is to develop capable, contributing citizens.[25]

This is not to say that colleges and universities shouldn't be interested in the successful employment of graduates. They are interested. That is why a college education is designed as it is. The reason college graduates obtain higher-paying jobs and have lower unemployment is not merely because students learn skills specific to certain jobs. Most vocational skills programs can do that in a matter of months. Rather, as a means of developing the capacities of citizens, college develops the kinds of people who will be able to be successful in whatever field of employment they choose. This broad focus is not as concerned with what graduates know how to do as with how they think and participate in the world. That is why a general education curriculum exists. That is why writing is stressed across disciplines. That is why universities require broad learning across all fields of study in addition to deep learning in a specific major.

In contrast, job training's significantly narrower focus primarily develops skill sets in shorter periods of time that are largely external to you—job skills that are mainly developed through practice and routine. Knowledge specifically related to professional skills is tied to particular industries and technologies that continually evolve, often making some of today's skills obsolete for tomorrow's world.

Still, vocational training programs provide many excellent opportunities for post-secondary training in important fields. Such programs are very good avenues for building a career. And not everyone has to go to college to get a good job or earn a good wage, though everyone needs some education or training after high school. My point, rather, is that for those who choose to attend college, it is essential to understand that the purpose of a college education is significantly different than that of job training.

Turning away from a primary focus on job training won't hinder your ability to develop professional knowledge and successfully compete for employment after college graduation. If you decide to embrace college's approach to developing broadly educated, capable citizens, do you have any reason to assume that you wouldn't be a successful job candidate? Becoming a learner and obtaining professional skills are not mutually exclusive choices. You don't choose one or the other. You simply need to let your preparation to become a contributing citizen give meaning and purpose to your learning so you can take full advantage of your education.

"I have to go to college if I want to have a good life."

As a college student you are undoubtedly concerned about the impact of your education on your future social and economic well-being. It is true that if you don't complete a degree, you will not have the same access to many of the higher-paying jobs available to college graduates. Therefore, you may have fewer opportunities for socio-economic progress. Certainly with less income over a lifetime, this may be the case.

The problem with this conversation is that it can turn education into an obligation instead of an opportunity. In other words, you *have* to go to college to reach your goals. Regardless of whether or not you feel that you have to go to college, there are significant problems with approaching your education as an obligation.

College is not a time to take for granted. The opportunities presented to you in college will open up paths in life that you could not have had otherwise. Your years in college will come and go. Whether you view this relatively short season of your life as an obligation or as an opportunity will have a significant influence on what you choose to do and who you become.

Talking about college and learning as an obligation can lead you to view your opportunity for education with indifference, causing you to feel frustrated by the amount of time and effort required for something that doesn't seem to have much intrinsic, personal value. As a result, your college education becomes an obstacle—something to get through and get over with. In short, you begin to lose ownership over your learning, and everything about your education that contributes to your personal development is seen as a burden.

Indifference can make doing the least amount of work at minimal quality and with little effort seem like a good idea. Thus, viewing education as an obligation can create habits and attitudes that can cause you to become less of a learner at the end of college than you were when you started.

On the other hand, talking about college and learning as an opportunity—regardless of the level of obligation you may feel—opens you to a level of learning that significantly influences who you become. You approach your education with a gratitude that recognizes the value and possibilities of learning. This perspective generates the energy you need to do the best work possible in order to maximize your personal development.

When you stop viewing college as an obstacle, you are ready to learn. And that learning then becomes a journey in which you have ownership. In this journey it's the process that matters most, and the ultimate and most important outcome is you. Therefore, you will work to overcome obstacles, seek challenges, and make up for the shortcomings of your circumstances.

"I'm paying for this, so it better be good."

The quality of your education is extremely important. Given the ever-increasing cost of tuition, the extremely high prices of textbooks, and the overall expense of a college education, you have every right to expect that college be a valuable and worthwhile experience. You want to get as much as you can for the significant amount of money and time you are investing.

However, it is important that you recognize exactly what you are purchasing. Yes, in college you will pay tuition and fees, and you will purchase textbooks and supplies. But what you are actually paying for is *access* and *opportunity;* you are not purchasing an education. It's similar to purchasing a membership to a gym. You are not a consumer of fitness and strength. You purchase access to the gym equipment and to people who can help you reach those goals *if* you do your part.

Likewise, you're not a consumer of higher education. Many people speak about making sure that you get a good "return on investment" when you go to college. But what does that mean? Most often it's talked about in terms of money spent. Your investment, however, isn't really money; at least paying for college won't get you anything because you are only paying for access and opportunity. Just like paying for a gym membership and buying the appropriate workout clothes won't make you stronger or healthier. Your real investment is time, energy, effort, and hard work. That's what gives you a return on your financial investment, and that return is largely dependent on you. Therefore, I encourage you to think of yourself as an apprentice—someone who's learning to learn under the guidance of others.

Approaching college and learning as something you're purchasing will significantly decrease your ability to become a learner. Those who view college from a consumer standpoint see teaching as a delivery method that doesn't necessarily require personal commitment and responsibility on the part of the learner. They expect teachers to be entertainers and believe that learning is always supposed to be fun.[26] In addition, consumers tend to be impatient; they want to be satisfied quickly. And they place the responsibility for quality on others.

Approaching college and learning as an apprenticeship, on the other hand, enables you to recognize that becoming is a steady process that takes time. When you see yourself as an apprentice, you will recognize your lack of knowledge and ability and, as a result, take the responsibility to sacrifice, study hard, and develop new capacities. You'll recognize that you need mentors and understand that learning includes developing relationships that require your personal commitment.

Too many students don't have the mindset of an apprentice. Instead, they sit back and expect to be taught. And some college professors may even reinforce this view. Still, you make college a valuable experience when you realize that the quality of your education depends on recognizing and taking responsibility for your steady development as a learner. You are not in college to buy something; you are there to become something.

"I just need to get that piece of paper."

The diploma you receive when you graduate from college is important. It's a valuable credential that enables you to be considered for various kinds of employment or graduate-level study and training. Because of this, people often say things like, "I just need to get that piece of paper" when they talk about persisting to graduation. Or sometimes when they are frustrated or disillusioned with college they will say, "I can't believe I have to do all this work for a piece of paper."

Talking like this might seem to make sense because the diploma is the tangible evidence that you receive to certify that you completed your degree. But talking this way also makes it seem as if your diploma has some value in and of itself that is independent of you.

It is a piece of paper. And it's an important piece of paper. But it is simply not true that everyone who has a diploma is somehow the same, with similar skills, abilities, knowledge, understanding, character, and work ethic. A diploma only certifies that you have met the minimum requirements for earning a bachelor's degree. It says nothing about the kind of learner you are, what your potential is, and what your abilities are.

Thinking that you just need "a piece of paper" will keep you from focusing on your personal development and your ability to learn. Instead, I suggest you focus on what a diploma is actually supposed to tell someone: That you have become a broadly educated person. Your diploma signals to others that you know how to learn and are capable of thinking carefully about the complexities of the world and solving difficult problems.

If you just focus on getting that piece of paper, you'll likely end up striving for minimum requirements, doing the least amount of work possible, and missing the opportunity to become an educated person. In a job interview, it's not your diploma that does the talking.

It's you. You're being evaluated as an educated person: how you think, communicate, and work. When you're on the job or working in your community, your diploma doesn't do anything. You do. It's your work and your education that informs what you do.

Therefore, the excitement and energy at your graduation will not be because you have "a piece paper" that tells the world you graduated from college. The enthusiasm of those who will be cheering for you as you walk across the stage to get your diploma will be because your education has hopefully made you a more capable, competent, and educated person than when you started. Who you are will influence what you can do, not the diploma.

"In the real world..."

We often talk about what we do outside the university or what we are going to do after graduation as what we will do "in the real world." You have probably used that phrase yourself. The problem is that when we assume there is a "real world," we are also assuming there is a fake world.

Certainly your future work, hobbies, and other activities will not look like a university campus or college classroom. Unless you become a professor, life after graduation will place you in circumstances that are very different than what you experience in college. However, the assumption that whatever awaits you out there is the "real world" can lead to a perception that what you do in college doesn't matter. If college isn't the real world, then why should you care about what you do or how you do it?

It's important to be excited about the prospect of graduation and moving on to different kinds of work and activities that may be more appealing to you. Looking forward to those opportunities and experiences will help keep you motivated during difficult and challenging times.

However, referring to life outside of college as the real world ignores the reality that you need to become a learner and a person of character as a result of your education. And you need to work on becoming that person now. I know many professors who understand how important it is to develop these qualities. So, for instance, they will not accept late assignments because a future employer certainly wouldn't accept late work. When students protest this policy, they often say, "Well, in the real world, my work wouldn't be late. I'd turn it in on time."

Graduation will not suddenly turn you into a responsible person who knows how to organize time, juggle competing priorities, and prepare quality work in time to meet deadlines. In addition, if you avoid your professors and classmates, never addressing disagreements or seeking to develop any kind of working relationship with them, you can't expect that "in the real world" you'll be able to directly address conflicts with your boss or be able to work well with colleagues, neighbors, or even family members. You must learn how to internalize these qualities now. This is the kind of preparation that will determine your character and who you will become.

Therefore, you must recognize that college *is* the real world. It won't be your world forever, but for a few years it's as real as anything you will ever experience.

In fact, if there is anything fake about college life, it's that it is a much safer place to make mistakes. Here, the consequences for mistakes are minor; you can learn from them and move on. For example, it's safer to learn how to deal with conflict and differences with professors and peers here than it is to learn those skills when you are in your first job with a boss and coworkers. Learning to seek feedback in order to improve the quality of your work and to increase your learning can be done with minimal risk compared to developing this ability on your first big project after college.

You can use every day in college to build your character and augment your capacity to learn independently. What you do and how you do it matters—it is real, and it has real consequences for who you become.

"When I'm done with school…"

For obvious reasons it's easy to see graduation as an end and a moment when your education is complete. I certainly thought of it that way when I was an undergraduate. Before I ever stepped foot on campus as a freshman, I had my education planned out: I would complete bachelor's and master's degrees. I was sure that when I reached that point every company would want to hire me because of my cutting-edge knowledge and skills. The problem wasn't my excitement and confidence; the problem was with how I saw myself when I finished college—complete. I somehow thought that when I graduated I would have everything I needed to be independently successful in my career. I was naïve.

Upon graduating, it isn't your knowledge or skills that make you valuable. In fact, you will very likely be the least qualified and experienced person when you start your first job. It's a lesson that every college graduate quickly learns. Therefore, your greatest value lies in your potential, your character, and knowing how to learn.

Yes, graduation is an ending point, but it is only the end of formal, classroom education. Graduation is also a new start. In fact, the graduation ceremony is called "commencement," which means a beginning. When you graduate you begin a new season of life where knowing how to learn becomes your greatest asset and the primary means by which you will achieve success. In most cases the depth and intensity of your learning will increase significantly after graduation.

Seeing yourself as complete or independently successful upon graduation makes learning seem like something you need to do in order to get to your intended goal rather than the vehicle that will carry you through all of life's endeavors. It's good to dream about finishing college and to imagine your success. But rather than dreaming about what you will know when you are finished with college, picture who you will become as the result of your quest for learning.

So the question is this: Will you become a capable learner by the time you graduate? Or will you still have to figure that out in personal, professional, and community circumstances where people will expect you to already be one?

Faulty Perspectives

Can you see how the conversations described above distract you, limiting your ability to understand the full possibilities of a college education? Embracing these faulty perspectives in your everyday conversations will prevent you from becoming a learner and reaching your potential. It will hinder your ability to take full advantage of the opportunities for personal growth and development that college affords. If you find yourself talking this way, change your conversation to focus more fully on your learning and who you are becoming. If you see others making decisions based on these faulty assumptions, kindly help them see the half-truths in their perspective that limit their learning.

In the next chapter I suggest a set of principles that will help you develop the abilities and character of a learner.

CHAPTER 4

Principles of Learning

When you understand the importance of becoming a learner, you'll be able to recognize and apply principles of learning that are often overlooked. Below, I offer seven principles for you to consider. They expand upon a number of ideas described in the previous chapters, and while not an exhaustive list, they offer more productive ways of thinking and talking about college and learning. Applying these principles will help you focus on who you are becoming.

Principle 1: The Most Important Things You Learn Will Not Be Graded

For most of my undergraduate education, I thought good grades and a diploma were the primary outcomes of college. Grades were most often the only way my success in learning was communicated to me. It was easy to get caught up in grades because that's how progress is assessed. Even so, like so many others, I quickly learned that it was possible to get an A on an assignment or in a class and yet learn very little. I also realized that I could get a B or C and learn a lot. In other words, I learned that it was shortsighted to see grades as the *full* measure of my success.

After I understood that the most important outcome of college was who I became, I could see that education has both immediate and lasting benefits. Immediate results are grades. Lasting effects are the characteristics we develop as a result of our learning. Both are important. However, we too often get so caught up in the pursuit of grades that we don't recognize that we can also develop ourselves in ways that are never formally assessed.

Your performance on exams, papers, and other assignments is only part of your education. How you study, the way you participate in class, the ways in which you seek help and feedback, how you deal with mistakes and failures, how you interact with teachers and classmates, how you overcome challenges and obstacles, how you deal with differences and conflict, and a host of other matters are the lasting outcomes of your education. Learning is a journey where the process is more important than the outcome.

Please don't misunderstand: Grades are important. Admission to academic majors, scholarships, internships, first jobs, and acceptance to graduate school all take grades into careful consideration. You should strive for good grades. But a primary emphasis on successful learning, especially when done carefully following the guidance, instruction, and mentorship of your teachers, should lead to good grades. That's the relationship between learning and grades that works. Even if the grade isn't as high as you like, some learning still took place. But when grades are more important than the process of learning, you miss out on the full learning opportunity.

Long after you have forgotten the details of what you've learned, the way you have developed yourself through your ability to be an independent learner will stay with you. This is because learning is a way of being. It is a part of your character; it's not just information that you have memorized.

Grades are used for indicating your abilities at very specific points in time. Within a few years after starting a career, grade point average becomes less and less important. The concerns of those evaluating you will shift away from grades and instead focus on your professional development and the kind of person you are.

Principle 2: Knowledge Is Interconnected

Most current education systems are based upon a mass-production industrial model that was developed over 100 years ago. For instance, subjects and disciplines are broken down and separated. Students are produced in batches. Degree requirements are listed with check-off boxes that are marked when completed.[27] While this model is useful for getting millions of people through public and higher education systems, it is not in your best interest to be mass-produced.

One of the biggest problems with our education system is that students begin seeing knowledge and areas of learning as disconnected: Writing is seen to be relevant only for English classes; math isn't necessary outside of calculus; giving presentations should be reserved for speech classes.

I once heard a very smart student ask, "Is our grade based entirely on the papers we've written during the semester and the essay exam?" When told that he was correct, he said in frustration, "But why? This isn't a writing class!"

What this student didn't understand is that while college separates knowledge into disciplines and subjects, learning and functioning in society requires us to connect different types of knowledge in a variety of ways.

When you look at life holistically, you will see that knowledge and fields of study are interconnected. Every profession demands that you write well. The problems faced by businesses, communities, and governments are rooted in historical and political context. All fields require communication skills. And most, if not all, technological and scientific innovation is grounded in mathematics. To be a successful problem solver and to think carefully and critically about the world around you, you must be able to connect various fields of knowledge.

Your challenge then is to look past the separation of subjects and knowledge and look for interconnections. You need to find ways to intertwine knowledge within a useful context, whether that context is an internship, a volunteer activity, or on an interdisciplinary project you are completing for a number of classes. Seeking this kind of interconnected learning will prepare you to successfully work through the problems and challenges you will face in your personal and professional life.

Don't be fooled into thinking that you'll never need math or writing or some other subject in your future work. Don't make the mistake that a student initially made when I gave him feedback on his writing and suggested that he work harder to develop his writing skills:

"This doesn't really matter," he said. "I'm always going to work for myself, so I'm never going to have to write anything or put together a resume."

"What about writing proposals to get people to invest in your business?" I said. "What about the writing you'll have to do to describe what you do and why people should be interested in it? What if at some point you choose to work for someone else in order to get some experience?"

He looked at me for a moment and then said, "I'd never really thought about that."

He then started thinking about those interconnections. And you should too.

Principle 3: You Must Take Responsibility for Your Learning

When we realize that education is about becoming a capable thinker and problem solver, we begin to think differently about our responsibility as learners. When I was focused on learning job skills, I saw my education as a body of knowledge and set of skills that were being given to me. I entered a classroom expecting the teacher to provide that knowledge and those skills. When that did not occur as I expected, I became frustrated because I'd given the responsibility for my education to my teacher.

Let me illustrate with an experience that cost me some valuable learning. After the first two weeks of an editing class, I was very disappointed in my professor. We hadn't received a complete syllabus, and she wouldn't commit to specific due dates for assignments. When asked, she simply said that our assignment was due sometime the next week. It took nearly a month to get a syllabus, and we rarely discussed the assigned readings in class. Needless to say I was not impressed. Some of my classmates and I complained that we weren't learning very much.

The last day of class we turned in our final projects and filled out a sheet that asked us to indicate how much of the reading we'd completed. I hadn't read much since we'd never discussed the readings in class. To my surprise, however, I overheard several students say they had done all the reading. I saw these same students turn in excellent projects. I felt a bit awkward about my mediocre efforts, but I felt somewhat justified because of the teacher's lack of organization and guidance. When the semester ended and grades were posted, I received a B. It was a generous grade. I remember complaining to my roommates and family: "I got a B in that class because I had a B teacher."

The next semester I ran into several classmates, and I complained again. Most felt the same way I did, but several of them had received an A. They said that despite the problems, they had learned some valuable things. At that point I felt embarrassed that I hadn't been able to overcome the difficulties and learn successfully. I wondered how some of my peers could learn and get high grades when, in my estimation, the class was taught poorly.

The answer is now painfully clear: I wasn't a learner. I was passive and didn't take responsibility for my education. I waited for explicit instructions. I wanted the teacher to tell me exactly what I needed to do to get an A. I wanted her to give me the knowledge I needed so I could give it back on a test. I made excuses for not learning.

Learners take responsibility for their learning. They thrive in classes despite poor teaching or other obstacles. No matter what kind of teacher you have, no matter what kind of class you are taking, if you are a learner you will set out to understand the material and create opportunities for success. As a learner you understand that when you blame others for a lack of learning, you only hurt yourself.

My professor moved on to the next semester, the next project, and the next class. My lack of learning didn't affect her at all. I moved on too but without the learning and knowledge that I needed. When I took a technical writing class the following semester and subsequently served an internship as a copy editor, I had to relearn the material I should have mastered in her class—doing everything on the fly.

Later, when my perspective shifted to becoming a learner, taking responsibility for my education came naturally. I made sure I got the help that I needed, looked for opportunities to be successful, and did not leave my learning in the hands of a teacher. Learning changed from something that was given to me in a classroom to an exercise in being a proactive, engaged, and responsible learner.

You too need to decide to be proactive, engaged, and responsible for your learning. The education you pursue is uniquely your own; it doesn't belong to anyone else.

Principle 4: Learning Requires a Relationship

When you become a learner, you recognize that you need to build strong, professional relationships and that you need to find mentors. You cannot become excellent at anything by simply reading books and taking tests. You need to learn from people who have experience in the subjects you are studying. This doesn't mean, however, that your professor has to become your best friend and hang out at your apartment. You don't want that and neither does your professor. What you do need is an appropriate professional relationship that enables you to feel comfortable asking questions, getting additional help, and receiving feedback on your work.

You also need to build connections with your peers. You will increase your ability to learn and be successful when you surround yourself with classmates who also want to be learners. Your peers can help you study, review your work, answer questions, and provide encouragement. Connecting with others in your classes will help you attend regularly and provide networking opportunities both now and after graduation.

Colleges and universities are set up in a way that can make it seem like there's no need for building relationships with professors and peers. You can sit in large lecture halls or in the back row and go through class without ever developing a relationship with your teacher or classmates.

I often have students come to me to ask for letters of recommendation. After their request many will say something like this: "You're the only teacher that really knows anything about me." This is regrettable, especially when this statement comes from a junior or senior. To be successful and to become who you need to become, you must develop working relationships with your teachers.

Unfortunately, most students work very hard to avoid any kind of relationship with their professors. Consider the following scenario: You wake up and go into the kitchen to grab a bite of breakfast on your way to class. You say good morning to your roommate and ask how she's doing. On your way out the door you thank another roommate for cleaning the living room. You catch the shuttle to campus and say good morning to the driver and thank him when you get off. When you enter the building, you say thanks to the person in front of you who holds open the door. As you enter the classroom, you exchange greetings with your classmates. Your professor is standing at the front of the room doing a few last-minute preparations. As you find your seat you don't look at your professor—no hello or good morning greeting. In fact, hardly anyone greets the professor. When class starts everyone sits quietly, listens, and takes notes. At times the professor waits in silence for someone to answer a question. When the class ends, the chatter among classmates rises as you all gather your stuff and leave. You walk out past the professor without making eye contact, offering a thank you, or saying anything else. Most of your peers do the same.

Isn't it ironic that we find it so easy to thank shuttle drivers and strangers who hold open doors, but then don't offer any thanks to someone who has spent an hour or more teaching us—not to mention the time it took to prepare for class and provide feedback on our work? Isn't it ironic that we offer pleasant and polite greetings to roommates and classmates, but we walk in and out of a classroom without making any effort to talk with or even acknowledge the professor? I know every student doesn't behave this way, but my experience both as a student and as a professor indicates that the general process I have described is not an exception—it's the general rule.

The problem with this scenario is that if you deal with your teachers this way, you are cutting yourself off from the very people who have the expertise and abilities to help you succeed. I understand that developing a working relationship with your professors can seem intimidating. It's a new relationship that is different than those you've had with high school teachers. You may worry about letting your professors know that you don't understand something. Some professors may come off as uninviting.

Still, students who have developed polite, respectful, pleasant, and professional relationships with their professors feel comfortable going to their offices and asking for help. They are not afraid to ask questions and seek feedback, especially when they are struggling. Students who ignore these associations find it very difficult to ask a professor for help, especially if they need some special considerations.

When you develop good relationships with your professors, you then put yourself in a position to find a mentor in your specific area or field of study. At some point you will decide on a major, and you will need a professor with whom you can work closely.

It is these mentor relationships that will give you learning opportunities beyond the classroom. Learning beyond the classroom provides new challenges and opportunities that help you become who you want to become. If you only learn through classes, tests, and papers, you will not become the kind of learner you otherwise could be.

Take the time to meet your professors, introduce yourself, and get help. Seek out these relationships. Don't sit back and never say a word. Don't cut yourself off from a powerful learning tool—your professors who are already expert in a given field and whose job it is to help you learn.

Principle 5: Learners Are Courageous

Education philosopher Parker Palmer says that "education is a fearful enterprise."[28] Students, he explains, are "afraid of failing, of not understanding, of being drawn into issues they would rather avoid, of having their ignorance exposed or their prejudices challenged, of looking foolish in front of their peers."[29] Teachers are afraid too, he says. They are afraid of being judged, of classes going badly, and of not being able to reach their students.[30] Fear paralyzes learning, causing us to get so caught up in always knowing the right answers that we try to avoid the challenges that make learning exciting and worthwhile.

In order to get the most out of your education, you have to recognize that it is only by mastering difficult ideas, successfully completing challenging work, and stretching beyond your current abilities that you become something better than you are. Learners are not afraid of hard work and challenging situations because they understand that becoming requires stretching and growing. Learners understand that they need to be courageous.

Trying to find out who the easiest teachers are and which classes require the least amount of work hinders good learning and gives you fewer opportunities to become a learner. This is not to say that you can't make practical choices in your course selection given the amount of classes you are taking and the amount of work each requires. You might need to take easier classes in order to balance out a semester in which you have several challenging classes. However, your focus should always be on what your courses offer you in terms of opportunities for developing your abilities and potential. Learners focus on challenging and stretching themselves through their education instead of trying to get through as quickly and easily as possible.

However, you probably know people who, ironically, spend a lot of time and energy trying to do as little work as possible, hoping to avoid challenging situations. If you are not concerned about your personal development and if you see grades as the ultimate measure of your success, then this approach makes sense. Getting through and getting by without the "hassle" of worrying about your growth will lead you to seek the path of least resistance—which is also the path of least fulfillment and satisfaction.

Your responsibility is to seek the kind of courses and opportunities that will enable you to become intellectually fit and capable; you cannot develop those qualities on the path of least resistance. You need to develop a long-term perspective that embraces challenges, seeks new opportunities, and finds value in mastering difficult knowledge. And that requires courage.

Principle 6: Learning Requires Humility

Learning how to learn requires understanding that it's okay that you don't know all the answers. Your strength doesn't lie in whether or not you have all the right answers. Your strength lies in knowing how to ask good questions, think critically, and develop solutions.

I find it interesting how much effort we spend worrying about having the wrong answer. When I was in college I was always afraid of not knowing the answer. I was afraid of being wrong. Given the countless quizzes and exams and the grades that accompany them, it's no surprise that I would feel that way.

Yet we need to understand that professional and personal success is not dependent on always being right. Significant problems and challenges aren't solved with ready-made answers; they are solved by learners who can carefully think through problems and come up with wise solutions.

You should be more concerned about knowing *how* to find answers to questions. That is a central characteristic of being a learner.

My fear is that students are so afraid to be wrong that they lack the humility (and courage) to experiment, to make mistakes, and to ask questions. Frequently, students don't ask questions because they are afraid their questions are "dumb" or because they are afraid the professor will think they are dumb. Yet they don't know the answer or understand the topic; they need more information or explanation. But instead of asking, they just move on, and in the process they don't learn. I see this most often when students turn in written papers. Countless times a student has handed me a paper and said, "I hope this is right" or "I hope this is what you're looking for" and then quickly left.

If you are not sure what you are doing is right, then why not ask the professor for clarification before you begin your paper or as you're working on it—long before you turn it in?

When I've asked my students why they didn't ask for help or clarification, they typically express their fear of being wrong or seeming incompetent. But think of it this way: When is it in your best interest to have the professor know your mistake—before she grades your paper or afterwards?

I am impressed by students who strive to be learners by coming in with drafts of their papers, showing me their work, and asking what they can do to improve their manuscripts so they can meet my expectations. They learn more in the process. And they get better grades.

Humility allows you to be teachable and to learn from mistakes and failures. As a learner you see mistakes and failures as tools to help you learn and grow so that you can become more successful.

Paradoxically, humility also breeds confidence. When you are humble enough to ask questions and make mistakes, you become more confident in your abilities because this process helps you to do better work. And this process significantly increases your learning.

Be humble enough to seek help, ask questions, solicit feedback on your work, and make improvements. You are not in college because you know all the answers. You're in college precisely because there are a lot of things you don't know and need to learn.

It's okay to be a novice and to make mistakes. Being afraid to be wrong will keep you from doing great things. As one education critic has said, "If you're not prepared to be wrong, you'll never come up with anything original."[31]

Principle 7: Learning Cannot Be Cheated

When you are focused on who you are becoming, there is no possible way to see cheating in a positive light. Only a perspective that ignores the process of becoming can see cheating as acceptable. Research shows, however, that over half of all college students cheat in some way.[32]

Each semester for the past several years I've had discussions with my students about honesty and integrity, and the topic of cheating always comes up. Many argue that cheating isn't a big deal. I remember one such discussion where at least half of the students passionately argued that while they knew cheating was bad, some cheating was excusable; it all depended on the context. They said that if they cheated on something small—like a quiz—then it really wasn't a problem because it didn't overly influence the final grade. If, however, they cheated on a paper by plagiarizing, then they saw that as a bigger problem because they were stealing someone else's work and trying to bypass a major assignment. When I asked these students how many of their peers regularly cheated on small things, the numbers ranged from 70 to 90 percent.

This conversation revealed that many students aren't aware that any kind of cheating—no matter how small—damages their ability to learn. More importantly, it damages their character.

Students who cheat have lost their vision. They've forgotten that their purpose in college is to become learners; it's not just about getting good grades. If you think that grades are all that matter, then cheating can make sense. But grades aren't what really matter in the long run.

If you are a learner, you will have a long-term perspective. You will know, for example, that if you cheat—even in seemingly small ways—and do it in class after class, semester after semester, you will become a cheater. You will become the kind of person who always seeks a way to cut corners, avoid responsibility, and not do what is expected. You will understand that becoming someone like that will negatively impact every facet of your life now and in the future.

The larger issue at stake is your integrity.

Throughout your college career you make and keep commitments. In particular, you agree to follow your school's standard of academic integrity—namely to do your own work and not cheat. Because you are continually in the process of fulfilling such commitments, you have the opportunity to develop your integrity on a daily basis. Cheating not only short-circuits learning, it also destroys rather than builds integrity. In addition, your integrity will be a central feature of your success in your family, community, and profession.

CHAPTER 5
An Invitation

This book is about change. And that change is based on understanding a simple but often overlooked idea: *The primary purpose of college isn't learning a specific set of professional skills; the primary purpose of college is to become a learner.*

There's perhaps no better way to improve your college experience than to understand that it's not just the accumulation of classes and grades and the earning of a degree that matter when you finish college. What matters most is the overall effect those experiences and achievements have on the kind of person you've become.

Admittedly, higher education has many problems that can affect your ability or opportunity to become a learner; most of these are out of your control. For example, large class sizes and sprawling campuses often make learning feel impersonal. Rising tuition and textbook costs increase your financial burdens. Many classes seem to encourage memorization more than inspire you to engage in meaningful learning. And sometimes professors are better scholars than they are teachers.

However, my purpose isn't to suggest that you have to have a perfect learning environment or be a perfect learner in every situation. Rather, you need to consistently strive to become a learner in all of your classes and activities. As you work to become a learner, you'll be able to focus on those things that you can influence and control, those things that will enable you to create for yourself an excellent education despite any shortcomings in your circumstances.

In other words, you don't have to have a perfect learning experience or be a perfect learner in college to reach your potential. It's who you become as a result of that process—no matter how imperfect your efforts or that process may be—that matters most. And since you will never have perfect circumstances in your community, profession, and relationships, becoming a learner in a less-than-ideal college situation can prepare you for solving problems and succeeding in this less-than-ideal world.

Putting These Ideas into Action

Every person experiences education differently. Our experiences, interests, preparation, abilities, and opportunities vary so much that it's impossible to tell anyone exactly how to pursue a college education in every detail. As I stated in the beginning, my intent isn't to offer a step-by-step, how-to guide for college success. Rather, my hope is that by helping you to focus on who you are becoming as a result of your education, you will more clearly see the crucial learning that you might otherwise overlook.

However, it's not good enough to simply read this book and think, "Well, that learning philosophy was interesting." You need to do something with these ideas.

Your challenge and opportunity is to carefully consider the idea that the primary outcome of a college education is the person you become. You must figure out how this knowledge can improve your education and how you can adapt it to your own needs, circumstances, goals, and field of study. To take full advantage of the opportunity of your education, you need to thoughtfully examine your assumptions about college and learning, identify the ways some of your assumptions hinder your ability to become a learner, and recognize the areas in which you've already been successful.

I invite you to carefully consider the ideas I have presented and begin to create your own philosophy of learning, outlining the specific ways you will strive to become a learner. Doing so will help you make sense of higher education's many opportunities and challenges. The following questions can help you begin this process:

- Outside of professional job skills, what learning abilities do I want to develop during college? How will I go about learning them?

- In what ways will I take better advantage of general education classes, especially if I am not necessarily interested in the topic?

- What is my plan to develop productive, professional relationships with my professors?

- What will I do when I find myself in a learning environment that I find difficult or challenging?

- How will I evaluate my success in ways other than with my grades?

- What is my plan to improve my work ethic and integrity during college?

- How will I deal with failures, setbacks, and obstacles?

And as you move from class to class and semester to semester, please consider the following questions to help you focus on and identify your individual progress as a learner:

- What are my learning goals for this class or semester? What will I do to achieve these goals?

- How does what I am learning in this class connect to what I am learning in other classes?

- How are my abilities to think critically, write effectively, solve problems, and communicate with others improving with this class or semester?

- What abilities and attributes am I developing in this class that will contribute to my future goals and help me be successful?

- What is something that I have struggled with in this specific class or semester? How did I overcome or deal with that challenge? What could I have done differently? How can I use that experience to improve?

- What is something really hard that I have done in this specific class or semester? How was I able to be successful? How can I replicate that in future classes and semesters?

Now, as you finish this book, please realize that this is not the end. It's the beginning of a new conversation. When you close this book, I hope you will take up this discussion with your peers, parents, and professors. Add your own stories and the stories of others. Find narratives that will help you remember and apply these ideas. Share what you've learned and teach others. Ask for feedback. Develop ideas and plans that will help you implement these principles in ways that best suit you. Then open the book again in challenging moments or before a new semester and review it to remind yourself again about the purpose and goals of higher education and how it can most benefit you. I am confident that you can use the ideas you've learned here as a lens through which you can continually make sense of and assess your opportunities, challenges, and successes.

Always remember: *The primary purpose of college is to become a learner.*

Acknowledgements

I am very grateful to the many people who have helped me develop and present the ideas found in this book. Without their various contributions, this book would not exist. First, I thank my wife, Julie, for her endless support and optimism as I have pursued this project. Her encouragement and feedback have been indispensable. I also thank my parents, Kemp and Janet Sanders, for their unwavering support and encouragement as I pursued my path in higher education.

I've been blessed with many kind mentors who helped me understand what it means to become a learner. Professor David Ward, whose literature class I write about in the introduction, played a crucial role in my life. I can point to his class as the pivotal moment in college when I began to think and learn differently. A conversation with Professor Scott Hammond about the news agency director was the catalyst for my realization that the purpose of college was to become a learner. His kind mentoring over several years sparked my love for teaching and gave me the confidence to pursue a PhD. In his graduate course, Professor Wayne Boss challenged me to pursue my goal to write this book. I thank each of these excellent professors.

A few people whom I do not know personally have influenced me as well. The various works of Parker J. Palmer, David A. Bednar, and Dallin H. Oaks have guided my thinking. Their writings led me to think about college—and life—as a process of becoming.

I am grateful to several people who helped me prepare the first edition of this book. Thanks to my students Coy Whittier and Jo Olsen for the many thoughtful conversations and brainstorming sessions. Thanks to Tyler Tolson, Jeff Sanders, Diane Ogden, Mike Zizzi, and Stephanie DeFilippis for their critical readings of this manuscript. And thank you to Janice LeFevre for her careful and excellent editing and Nathan Sanders for his excellent production and design work.

In addition, I express my appreciation to Noelle Call and Lisa Simmons at Utah State University for their support of my work and for giving me my first opportunity to share these ideas with a large audience of students. They set this whole project in motion.

Since the first edition of this book was published, I'm also indebted to many colleagues and mentors who expanded my knowledge, supported my work, and gave me opportunities to share my work with others. So thank you to Clair Canfield, Mitchell Culver, Norm Jones, Heidi Kesler, Harrison Kleiner, Kristina Scharp, and Gordon Steinhoff. I am also grateful for the many others who have introduced this book to their colleagues and students over the past several years.

Finally, I would like to thank Mike Howard, Barb DeVore, and all the design and production staff at Hayden-McNeil and Macmillan Learning for their excellent work on the second edition of this book.

Notes and Bibliography

Notes

Introduction

1. David Ward, from author's notes, January 1999.

Chapter 1

2. Scott Hammond, personal conversation with author, February 2002.

3. *It Takes More than a Major: Employer Priorities for College Learning and Student Success.* 2013. Washington, DC: Association of American Colleges and Universities and Hart Research Associates.

4. Valerie Strauss, "The Surprising Thing Google Learned about Its Employees—and What It Means for Today's Students," *Washington Post*, December 20, 2017.

5. Neil Postman, *The End of Education* (New York: Vintage Books, 1996), 27–33; Fareed Zakaria, *In Defense of a Liberal Education* (New York: Norton, 2015).

6. Michael Crow, "Is College Worth It?" January 21, 2015.

7. Paul Willis, *Learning to Labour: How Working Class Kids Get Working Class Jobs* (Farnborough, England: Saxon House, 1977), 185–192.

8. Michael S. Roth, *Beyond the University: Why Liberal Education Matters* (New Haven: Yale University Press, 2014), xv–xvi.

Chapter 2

9. Brian McCoy, "Success," *Vital Speeches of the Day* 73 (July 2007): 321–322.

10. *Declining by Degrees: Higher Education at Risk,* (PBS, 2005), DVD; Richard Arum & Josipa Roksa, *Academically Adrift: Limited Learning on College Campuses* (Chicago: University of Chicago Press, 2010); William Deresiewicz, *Excellent Sheep* (New York: Free Press, 2015).

11. Ken Robinson, "Ken Robinson Says Schools Kill Creativity," filmed 2006. *TED* video, 0:19.

12. Anthony Carnevale, Nicole Smith, and Jeff Strohl, "Help Wanted: Projections of Jobs and Education Requirements through 2018," June 2010, *Georgetown University: Center on Education and the Workforce.*

13. Peter C. Brown, Henry L. Roediger III, & Mark A. McDaniel, *Make It Stick: The Science of Successful Learning* (Cambridge, MA: Belknap Press, 2014), 28.

14. Peter Behrendt, class presentation at the University of Colorado at Boulder, April 2008.

15. For more information on this subject, see Chip Walter, "Kryder's Law," *Scientific American* [serial online], July 25, 2005, 32–33.

16. Ken Robinson, *The Element: How Finding Your Passion Changes Everything* (New York: Penguin Books, 2009), 67.

17. Robinson, "Ken Robinson Says Schools Kill Creativity."

18. Jim Collins, foreword to "The Highest Goal: The Secret that Sustains You in Every Moment," by Michael Ray, *JimCollins.com,* January 2004.

19. Robinson, *The Element,* 67–70.

20. Ben Clegg, personal conversation with author, June 2010.

21. Ken Bain, *What the Best College Teachers Do* (Cambridge, Massachusetts: Harvard University Press, 2004), 22–32.

22. National Association of Colleges and Employers (NACE), *Job Outlook 2012* (Bethlehem, Pennsylvania: NACE, 2011), 28.

Chapter 3

23. Dennis Romboy, "Utah Colleges Provide 'Degrees to Nowhere,' State Senator Says," *Deseret News*, February 1, 2011; Michael Stratford, "In GOP Debate, Rubio Again Criticizes Philosophy," *Inside Higher Ed*, November 11, 2015; Nick DeSantis, "Obama Questions Value of Art-History Degree," *Chronicle of Higher Education*, January 20, 2014.

24. Carnevale, Smith, and Strohl, "Help Wanted."

25. Neil Postman, *The End of Education* (New York: Vintage Books, 1996), 27–33.

26. Jill J. McMillan and George Cheney, "The Student as Consumer: The Implications and Limitations of a Metaphor," *Communication Education* 45, no. 1 (January 1996): 4–9.

Chapter 4

27. Robinson, "Ken Robinson Says Schools Kill Creativity."

28. Parker Palmer, *The Courage to Teach: Exploring the Inner Landscape of a Teacher's Life* (San Francisco: Jossey-Bass, 1998), 36.

29. Palmer, *The Courage to Teach*, 37.

30. Palmer, 36–38.

31. Robinson, "Ken Robinson Says Schools Kill Creativity."

32. Denise Nitterhouse, "Plagiarism—Not Just an Academic Problem," *Teaching Business Ethics* 7, no. 3 (August 2003): 216.

Bibliography

American Association of Colleges and Universities. *It Takes More than a Major: Employer Priorities for College Learning and Student Success.* Washington DC: Hart Research Associates, 2013.

Arum, Richard and Roksa, Josipa. *Academically Adrift: Limited Learning on College Campuses.* Chicago, Illinois: University of Chicago Press, 2010.

Bain, Ken. *What the Best College Teachers Do.* Cambridge, Massachusetts: Harvard University Press, 2004.

Brown, Peter C., Roediger III, Henry L., and McDaniel, Mark A. *Make It Stick: The Science of Successful Learning.* Cambridge, Massachusetts: Belknap Press, 2014.

Carnevale, Anthony, Nicole Smith, and Jeff Strohl. "Help Wanted: Projections of Jobs and Education Requirements through 2018." June 2010. *Georgetown University: Center on Education and the Workforce.* http://cew.georgetown.edu/jobs2018/.

Collins, Jim. Foreword to "The Highest Goal: The Secret that Sustains You in Every Moment," by Michael Ray. *JimCollins.com.* January 2004. http://www.jimcollins.com/article_topics/articles/the-highest-goal.html.

Crow, Michael. "Is College Worth It?" Speech given January 21, 2015. https://president.asu.edu/node/1454.

Declining by Degrees: Higher Education at Risk. (PBS, 2005). DVD.

Deresiewicz, William. *Excellent Sheep: The Miseducation of the American Elite.* New York: Free Press, 2015.

DeSantis, Nick. "Obama Questions Value of Art-History Degree." *Chronicle of Higher Education.* January 20, 2014. https://www.chronicle.com/blogs/ticker/obama-questions-value-of-art-history-degrees/72073.

McCoy, Brian. "Success." *Vital Speeches of the Day* 73 (July 2007): 321–322. http://connection.ebscohost.com/c/speeches/25571246/success.

McMillan, Jill J., and George Cheney. "The Student as Consumer: The Implications and Limitations of a Metaphor." *Communication Education* 45, no. 1 (January 1996): 1–15.

National Association of Colleges and Employers (NACE). *Job Outlook 2012*. Bethlehem, Pennsylvania: NACE, 2011.

Nitterhouse, Denise. "Plagiarism—Not Just an Academic Problem." *Teaching Business Ethics* 7, no. 3 (August 2003): 215–227.

Palmer, Parker. *The Courage to Teach: Exploring the Inner Landscape of a Teacher's Life*. San Francisco: Jossey-Bass, 1998.

Postman, Neil. *The End of Education*. New York: Vintage Books, 1996.

Robinson, Ken. *The Element: How Finding Your Passion Changes Everything*. New York: Penguin Books, 2009.

———. "Ken Robinson Says Schools Kill Creativity." Filmed 2006. *TED* video, 0:19. http://www.ted.com/talks/lang/en/ken_robinson_says_schools_kill_creativity.html.

Romboy, Dennis. "Utah Colleges Provide 'Degrees to Nowhere,' State Senator Says." *Deseret News*. February 1, 2011. https://www.deseretnews.com/article/705365648/Utah-colleges-provide-degrees-to-nowhere-state-senator-says.html.

Roth, Michael. *Beyond the University: Why Liberal Education Matters*. New Haven, Connecticut: Yale University Press, 2014.

Stratford, Michael. "In GOP Debate, Rubio Again Criticizes Philosophy." *Inside Higher Ed*. November 11, 2015. https://www.insidehighered.com/quicktakes/2015/11/11/gop-debate-rubio-again-criticizes-philosophy.

Strauss, Valerie. "The Surprising Thing Google Learned About Its Employees—and What It Means for Today's Students." *Washington Post*. December 20, 2017. https://www.washingtonpost.com/news/answer-sheet/wp/2017/12/20/the-surprising-thing-google-learned-about-its-employees-and-what-it-means-for-todays-students/?utm_term=.dfa145373ed3.

Walter, Chip. "Kryder's Law." *Scientific American* [serial online]. July 25, 2005. http://www.scientificamerican.com/article. cfm?id=kryders-law.

Willis, Paul. *Learning to Labour: How Working Class Kids Get Working Class Jobs*. Farnborough, England: Saxon House, 1977.

Zakaria, Fareed. *In Defense of a Liberal Education*. New York: Norton, 2015.